THE FIRST
Really Important
SURVEY OF
AMERICAN
HABITS

by Mel Poretz and Barry Sinrod

PRICE STERN SLOAN
Los Angeles

DEDICATION

To Inez, my best friend in the world.
                              -MP

To my wonderful wife, Shelly, my children, Jodey, Marlo, Blake and my son-in law David. This quirky, loving family helped make this book possible.
                                                            -BS

Published by Price Stern Sloan, Inc.
360 North La Cienega Boulevard
Los Angeles, CA 90048

10 9 8 7 6 5 4 3

Library of Congress Catalog Card Number: 89-61373

ISBN 0-8431-2735-X

TABLE OF CONTENTS

STATISTICAL QUIRKS

Due to the fact that not everyone answered every question and some people chose more than one option per answer, some columns of figures may add to more or less than 100%. For example, only 73% of the females and 91% of the males answered the question "How old were you when you first made love?" In this case, the total columns add up to less than 100%. On the question, "What do you do when you can't sleep at night: toss, read, watch TV/listen to radio or other?" several participants indicated two or more choices. In this case, the total columns add up to more than 100%.

This variation of response also affects the balance between male and female totals because a disproportionate number of one sex may be answering the question. The following is an example tabulation for the question, "When you and your mate sign a greeting card, whose name goes first?"

	MALE	FEMALE	SURVEY
Total Responses For This Question	1,489	700	2,189
Total Responses For His Name First	1,020 (69%)	501 (72%)	1,521 (69%)

To find the grand totals, you'd be tempted to add 69% with 72% and divide by two giving you a grand total of 71%. However, the correct way of arriving at this figure is as follows.

$$\frac{\text{Males His Name First} + \text{Females His Name First}}{\text{Total Males} + \text{Total Females}}$$

$$\frac{1,020 + 501 = 1,521}{1,489 + 700 = 2,189} = 69\%$$

All totals are statistically correct and can be verified, trust us.

INTRODUCTION

We've always been compulsive, obsessive collectors of odd tidbits of information. How many people wear torn underwear under their expensive clothes? How many unmatched socks lie lonely in dresser drawers? Does everybody roll the toilet paper over the spool?

Since both of us had extensive backgrounds in marketing, we knew the truth about the seemingly insignificant habits of the American public was accessible through a survey. So, we decided to go directly to the source. As a test, we piggy-backed a small-scale survey of several thousand expectant mothers who were part of a national mail opinion panel then being conducted by the Sinrod Marketing Group. We were pleasantly surprised by the flood of new inconsequential questions, many of which are included in this book, volunteered by the mothers-to-be. From there we rolled out a nationwide survey to adults over 21 years of age.

The sample was developed from geographic patterns obtained from the United States Census Bureau. It included adult residents of each of the fifty states, each of the Standard Consolidated Statistical Areas (SCSA) and correct proportions of participants from the two hundred and fifty largest counties and cities and areas which are not a part of a larger metropolitan grouping but which have at least 2500 citizens. The sample represents 89% of the total adult population of the United States and has been statistically tested to be within a plus or minus 3% accuracy range.

We had a phenomenal response rate of 26% with 55% of our patriotic participants being female and 45% being male. You'll find other demographic features of the participants in the back of the book.

So we lay before you two lifetimes of curiosity satisfied (to some extent) at long last. If you harbor any imponderables, send them to:

Inconsequential Questions
P.O. Box 300
Westbury, NY 11590

Truth is stranger than fiction. And we've got the stats to prove it.

Mel Poretz	Barry Sinrod
The Fulfillment House, Inc.	Sinrod Marketing
Westbury, NY	Hicksville, NY

AMERICANS AND THE BEDROOM

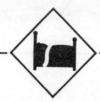

DO YOU SLEEP IN THE NUDE
OR IN PAJAMAS?

AGE	NUDE		PJ'S.	
	M	F	M	F
21-34	38	10	62	90
35-44	40	33	60	67
45-54	36	25	64	75
55 +	75	9	25	91
■ M □ F M/F TOTALS	41	21	59	79
GRAND TOTALS	31%		69%	

All numbers based on percentages.

Eighty-five percent of the respondents from the North and 65% of the folks down South wear pj's.

Eighty-five percent of the women who perceive themselves as over-weight told us they prefer pajamas.

DO YOU WEAR UNDERWEAR TO BED?

AGE	YES		NO	
	M	F	M	F
21-34	89	50	11	50
35-44	67	21	33	79
45-54	53	32	47	68
55 +	38	21	63	79
■ M □ F M/F TOTALS	54	27	46	73
GRAND TOTALS	39%		61%	

All numbers based on percentages.

WHAT IS YOUR FAVORITE SLEEPING POSITION?

AGE	SIDE		STOMACH		BACK	
	M	F	M	F	M	F
21-34	70	73	20	18	10	9
35-44	73	90	7	5	20	5
45-54	73	68	14	26	14	5
55 +	40	73	10	27	50	0
M/F TOTALS	71	78	8	20	21	2
GRAND TOTALS	76%		14%		10%	

All numbers based on percentages.

WHAT DO YOU DO
WHEN YOU CAN'T SLEEP AT NIGHT?

AGE	TOSS		READ		TV/RADIO		OTHER	
	M	F	M	F	M	F	M	F
21-34	50	62	16	12	31	9	3	17
35-44	53	50	18	33	13	10	16	7
45-54	38	50	14	15	38	15	10	20
55 +	44	36	20	36	21	18	15	9
■ M □ F M/F TOTALS	44	48	14	27	28	13	14	12
GRAND TOTALS	48%		22%		19%		12%	

All numbers based on percentages.

Any idea what "OTHER" might be?

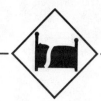

WHAT TIME DO YOU GO TO BED?

AGE	8-9		9-10		10-11		11-12		12 +	
	M	F	M	F	M	F	M	F	M	F
21-34	3	26	43	10	51	16	2	11	1	36
35-44	2	28	12	17	43	25	14	22	29	8
45-54	11	21	16	18	47	20	12	14	14	25
55 +	4	10	13	26	44	10	25	30	10	23

■ M
□ F

M/F TOTALS

	8-9		9-10		10-11		11-12		12 +	
M/F TOTALS	5	20	18	19	48	20	12	19	12	20
GRAND TOTALS	**13%**		**18%**		**35%**		**15%**		**16%**	

All numbers based on percentages.

ONCE YOUR ALARM GOES OFF, WHAT DO YOU DO?

AGE	GET UP		DELAY BUTTON		SLEEP	
	M	F	M	F	M	F
21-34	59	50	37	25	4	25
35-44	52	36	41	43	·7	21
45-54	54	56	35	33	12	11
55+	36	33	51	33	13	33
■ M □ F M/F TOTALS	54	48	37	34	10	18
GRAND TOTALS	51%		35%		13%	

All numbers based on percentages.

Forty-three percent of the white-collar workers press the delay button, while only 21% of the blue-collar workers do.

HOW OLD WERE YOU...

AGE	UNDER 13		13-15		16		17	
	M	F	M	F	M	F	M	F
21-34	0	0	0	2	8	17	27	25
35-44	4	2	7	8	20	17	16	13
45-54	11	0	20	8	22	26	12	19
55 +	0	2	6	14	18	14	20	17
M ⬛ F ⬜ M/F TOTALS	6	2	10	6	18	19	18	18
GRAND TOTALS	3%		11%		19%		18%	

All numbers based on percentages.

...WHEN YOU FIRST MADE LOVE?

AGE	18		19		20		21+	
	M	F	M	F	M	F	M	F
21-34	33	30	26	16	3	5	3	5
35-44	14	15	7	6	12	14	20	25
45-54	7	9	4	3	6	11	18	24
55+	26	20	11	10	9	14	10	9
■ M ☐ F M/F TOTALS	17	20	9	10	7	10	15	15
GRAND TOTALS	17%		9%		7%		15%	

All numbers based on percentages.

DID YOU ENJOY
THE FIRST TIME YOU MADE LOVE?

AGE	YES		NO	
	M	F	M	F
21-34	99	50	1	50
35-44	85	55	15	45
45-54	84	37	16	63
55 +	99	47	1	53
M/F TOTALS ▪ M □ F	86	41	14	59
GRAND TOTALS	68%		32%	

All numbers based on percentages.

Seventy-six percent of the Westerners enjoyed their introduction to lovemaking, more than any other geographical category.

Seventy-three percent of the white-collar workers liked their first sexual experience, as did 63% of the blue-collar workers.

Ninety-one percent of the men who perceive themselves as overweight were pleased with their first sexual experience; however, 34% of the women who perceive themselves as overweight were not. In fact, these women enjoyed it least of all the female groupings (34%).

DID YOU LEARN THE FACTS OF LIFE FROM YOUR PARENTS OR FRIENDS?

AGE	PARENTS		FRIEND	
	M	F	M	F
21-34	6	33	94	67
35-44	17	14	83	86
45-54	5	21	95	79
55 +	50	18	50	82
■ M □ F M/F TOTALS	16	20	84	80
GRAND TOTALS	19%		81%	

All numbers based on percentages.

Ninety-one percent of the Easterners and 74% of the Westerners got the "facts" from their buddies rather than from a "heart-to-heart" talk at home.

For those respondents earning $20K or less, it was 50%-50%, and for those earning $50K or more, it was 17% parents and 83% friends.

WHAT IS YOUR FAVORITE TIME TO HAVE SEX?

AGE	AM		AFTER-NOON		EVENING		AFTER MIDNIGHT	
	M	F	M	F	M	F	M	F
21-34	33	14	8	13	57	53	2	20
35-44	9	4	18	40	69	38	4	18
45-54	46	20	8	9	38	53	8	18
55+	41	51	5	9	43	30	11	10
■ M □ F M/F TOTALS	32	21	10	16	52	49	6	14
GRAND TOTALS	26%		13%		50%		11%	

All numbers based on percentages.

With whom are all those post-midnight women (14%) having sex—obviously not the men (6%)!

WHAT OTHER THINGS ARE TURNED ON WHEN YOU MAKE LOVE?

AGE	LIGHTS		MUSIC		TV		ALL		NONE	
	M	F	M	F	M	F	M	F	M	F
21-34	2	57	1	3	42	10	38	20	17	10
35-44	13	16	6	5	26	27	38	32	17	20
45-54	19	21	4	16	25	22	42	27	10	14
55 +	50	20	1	42	2	1	30	22	17	15
M/F TOTALS	21	29	2	16	24	15	38	25	15	15
GRAND TOTALS	25%		10%		20%		30%		15%	

All numbers based on percentages.

Twenty-one- to thirty-four-year-old men are just as interested in M*A*S*H as M*U*S*H; however, their lovers (and the 55 + men) just don't want to be left in the dark. The 55 + women like to make love to music.

AS A MAN, WHAT PART OF A WOMAN'S BODY DO YOU LOOK AT FIRST?

AGE	FACE	CHEST	EYES	LEGS	BEHIND
21-34	26	40	2	1	31
35-44	60	5	5	6	24
45-54	67	11	4	5	13
55 +	78	18	1	1	2
■M TOTALS	60%	21%	4%	4%	11%

All numbers based on percentages.

AS A WOMAN, WHAT PART OF A MAN'S BODY DO YOU LOOK AT FIRST?

AGE	FACE	MUSCLES	EYES	LEGS	BEHIND
21-34	38	7	15	5	35
35-44	68	4	12	5	11
45-54	73	7	16	2	2
55+	44	10	33	2	11
TOTALS	56	8	21	3	12

☐ F

All numbers based on percentages.

IF YOU SMOKE,
DO YOU SMOKE AFTER SEX?

AGE	YES		NO	
	M	F	M	F
21-34	33	50	67	50
35-44	19	33	81	67
45-54	29	21	71	79
55 +	2	2	98	98
M/F TOTALS	22	29	78	71
GRAND TOTALS	25%		75%	

All numbers based on percentages.

As we get older, it seems men, as well as women, have little energy left to do anything after sex.

ARE YOU IN FAVOR OF YOUR CHILDREN MARRYING AS VIRGINS?

AGE	YES		NO	
	M	F	M	F
21-34	89	67	11	33
35-44	89	67	11	33
45-54	52	68	48	32
55 +	83	60	17	40
■ M ☐ F M/F TOTALS	71	66	29	34
GRAND TOTALS	**69%**		**31%**	

All numbers based on percentages.

Eighty-nine percent of the participants who earn less than $20K favor virginity for their progeny. Fifty-seven percent of those who earn $50K or more prefer premarital experiences for their heirs and assigns.

AMERICANS AND
THEIR CLOTHES

IN WHICH SEQUENCE DO YOU PUT ON YOUR SOCKS AND SHOES?

AGE	SOCK-SOCK SHOE-SHOE		SOCK-SHOE SOCK-SHOE	
	M	F	M	F
21-34	73	90	27	10
35-44	75	75	25	25
45-54	83	79	17	21
55 +	75	90	25	10
■ M □ F M/F TOTALS	80	83	20	17
GRAND TOTALS	81%		19%	

All numbers based on percentages.

HOW MANY UNMATCHED SOCKS DO YOU HAVE IN YOUR DRAWER?

AGE	NONE		ONE		TWO		THREE		FOUR +	
	M	F	M	F	M	F	M	F	M	F
21-34	60	75	4	8	3	8	20	5	13	4
35-44	38	81	5	4	25	2	13	4	19	9
45-54	78	88	6	5	8	3	2	2	6	2
55 +	45	87	1	3	11	1	20	6	23	3
M/F TOTALS (■ M / □ F)	55	83	2	5	13	3	17	5	13	4
GRAND TOTALS	70%		3%		8%		10%		9%	

All numbers based on percentages.

IF ONE SOCK OF A PAIR HAS A HOLE, DO YOU MEND IT, TOSS IT AWAY OR TOSS AWAY THE PAIR?

AGE	MEND		TOSS SOCK		TOSS PAIR	
	M	F	M	F	M	F
21-34	47	5	48	31	5	64
35-44	6	38	38	19	56	43
45-54	24	14	38	28	38	58
55+	48	50	2	17	50	33
■ M □ F M/F TOTALS	21	24	35	25	44	51
GRAND TOTALS	23%		29%		48%	

All numbers based on percentages.

Thirty-three percent of those who earn $50K or more mend their socks; only 11% of those who earn under $20K do.

Only 4% of the college educated participants, as compared with 29% of the non-college educated participants, mend socks.

DO YOU STORE YOUR SOCKS ROLLED UP OR FOLDED FLAT?

AGE	ROLLED		FLAT	
	M	F	M	F
21-34	98	67	2	33
35-44	52	48	48	52
45-54	59	51	41	49
55 +	48	2	52	98
■ M □ F M/F TOTALS	57	47	43	53
GRAND TOTALS	51%		49%	

All numbers based on percentages.

DO YOU WALK AROUND
THE HOUSE BAREFOOT?

AGE	YES		NO	
	M	F	M	F
21-34	8	67	92	33
35-44	67	50	33	50
45-54	42	63	58	37
55 +	38	40	63	60
■ M ☐ F M/F TOTALS	44	56	56	44
GRAND TOTALS	50%		50%	

All numbers based on percentages.

WHEN DO YOU PLAN
WHAT YOU'LL WEAR THE NEXT DAY,
THE NIGHT BEFORE
OR THE NEXT MORNING?

AGE	NIGHT BEFORE		NEXT DAY	
	M	F	M	F
21-34	28	50	72	50
35-44	45	33	55	67
45-54	20	35	80	65
55 +	50	45	50	55
■ M □ F M/F TOTALS	31	38	69	62
GRAND TOTALS	35%		65%	

All numbers based on percentages.

DO YOU WEAR
COLORED UNDERWEAR?

AGE	YES		NO	
	M	F	M	F
21-34	21	98	79	2
35-44	25	65	75	35
45-54	25	82	75	18
55 +	2	80	98	20
■ M ☐ F	24	78	76	22
M/F TOTALS				
GRAND TOTALS	51%		49%	

All numbers based on percentages.

Sixty-two percent of the men who perceive themselves as overweight and 73% of Northerners consider white their favorite color (or non-color) of underwear, as do 44% of the Southerners.

WOULD YOU WEAR TORN UNDERGARMENTS?

AGE	YES		NO	
	M	F	M	F
21-34	65	99	35	1
35-44	64	63	36	38
45-54	71	42	29	58
55 +	50	55	50	45
■ M □ F **M/F TOTALS**	68	57	32	43
GRAND TOTALS	**61%**		**39%**	

All numbers based on percentages.

Forty-eight percent of the blue-collar workers would not wear torn underwear, while 74% of the white-collar workers would.

WHICH LEG DO YOU PUT INTO YOUR TROUSERS FIRST?

AGE	LEFT		RIGHT	
	M	F	M	F
21-34	49	40	51	60
35-44	58	50	42	50
45-54	50	26	50	74
55 +	25	36	75	64
■ M ☐ F / M/F TOTALS	51	35	49	65
GRAND TOTALS	42%		58%	

All numbers based on percentages.

DO YOUR TROUSERS HANG IN THE CLOSET FROM THE LEGS, FROM THE WAISTBAND OR FOLDED OVER A HANGER?

AGE	LEGS		WAIST		FOLDED	
	M	F	M	F	M	F
21-34	2	2	1	1	97	97
35-44	31	5	6	5	63	90
45-54	22	11	11	12	67	77
55 +	50	16	48	1	2	83
■ M ☐ F M/F TOTALS	28	9	10	8	62	83
GRAND TOTALS	16%		8%		76%	

All numbers based on percentages.

DO YOU OR YOUR MATE HAVE MORE CLOSET SPACE?

AGE	SELF		MATE	
	M	F	M	F
21-34	10	20	90	80
35-44	36	23	64	77
45-54	11	18	89	82
55+	11	27	89	73
■ M □ F **M/F TOTALS**	18	21	82	79
GRAND TOTALS	**20%**		**80%**	

All numbers based on percentages.

Who are these people married to?

IS YOUR PAPER MONEY KEPT IN ORDER OF DENOMINATION OR RANDOMLY?

AGE	DENOM.		RANDOM	
	M	F	M	F
21-34	90	75	10	25
35-44	61	64	39	36
45-54	80	77	20	23
55 +	80	90	20	10
■ M ☐ F M/F TOTALS	72	75	28	25
GRAND TOTALS	74%		26%	

All numbers based on percentages.

Eighty-three percent of the Southerners keep their money clipped nice and neat; only 69% of the Northerners do.

AMERICANS AND
THE BATHROOM

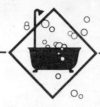

DO YOU PREFER THAT YOUR TOILET TISSUE UNWINDS OVER OR UNDER THE SPOOL?

AGE	OVER		UNDER	
	M	F	M	F
21-34	71	81	29	19
35-44	81	65	19	35
45-54	60	62	40	38
55 +	63	83	37	17
M (black) / F (white) **M/F TOTALS**	69	67	31	33
GRAND TOTALS	68%		32%	

All numbers based on percentages.

Sixty percent of those who earn $50K or more roll their paper over, while 73% of those who earn less than $20K do the opposite.

DO YOU REPLACE
AN EMPTY ROLL OF TOILET TISSUE OR
DO YOU LEAVE IT FOR
THE NEXT PERSON TO REPLACE?

AGE	REPLACE		LEAVE	
	M	F	M	F
21-34	96	97	4	3
35-44	78	96	22	4
45-54	94	82	6	18
55+	71	97	29	3
■ M □ F M/F TOTALS	83 / 91		17 / 9	
GRAND TOTALS	88%		12%	

All numbers based on percentages.

It seems most of us have some sense of compassion.

HAVING A CHOICE OF THREE UNOCCUPIED STALLS OR URINALS, WOULD YOU USE THE ONE ON THE LEFT, MIDDLE OR RIGHT?

AGE	LEFT		MIDDLE		RIGHT	
	M	F	M	F	M	F
21-34	1	31	98	65	1	4
35-44	30	45	36	30	34	25
45-54	20	26	45	29	35	45
55 +	54	50	2	17	44	33
■ M □ F M/F TOTALS	28	34	40	29	32	37
GRAND TOTALS	31%		34%		35%	

All numbers based on percentages.

Fifty-three percent of the Southern women opt for the middle stall, while only 25% of the Northern women do. Sixty percent of the Southern men go for the stall on the left, as do 40% of the Northern men.

Forty-four percent of those who earn $50K or more choose the middle stall. Fifty-five percent of those who earn less than $20K prefer to keep to the right.

IF THE STALL OR URINAL ON THE LEFT WAS OCCUPIED, WOULD YOU USE THE ONE NEXT TO IT OR THE ONE ON THE FAR RIGHT?

AGE	MIDDLE		RIGHT	
	M	F	M	F
21-34	2	34	98	66
35-44	31	49	69	51
45-54	18	29	82	71
55 +	48	35	52	65
■ M □ F M/F TOTALS	27	35	73	65
GRAND TOTALS	32%		68%	

All numbers based on percentages.

Fifty-four percent of the Southerners, as opposed to 28% of the Northerners, would choose the middle stall. The folks down South are friendly, aren't they?

DO YOU LOOK BEHIND THE SHOWER CURTAIN OR DOOR WHEN USING SOMEONE ELSE'S BATHROOM?

AGE	YES		NO	
	M	F	M	F
21-34	2	25	98	75
35-44	3	14	97	86
45-54	10	3	90	97
55 +	2	2	98	98
■ M □ F M/F TOTALS	6	8	94	92
GRAND TOTALS	7%		93%	

All numbers based on percentages.

DO YOU PREFER SHOWERING OR BATHING?

AGE	SHOWER		BATH	
	M	F	M	F
21-34	98	98	2	2
35-44	94	64	6	36
45-54	76	72	24	28
55+	99	83	1	17
■ M □ F M/F TOTALS	86	70	14	30
GRAND TOTALS	76%		24%	

All numbers based on percentages.

DO YOU SING
IN THE SHOWER (OR BATH)?

AGE	YES		NO	
	M	F	M	F
21-34	16	33	84	67
35-44	19	63	81	38
45-54	44	30	56	70
55 +	50	25	50	75
■ M □ F M/F TOTALS	33	40	67	60
GRAND TOTALS	38%		62%	

All numbers based on percentages.

Thirty-three percent of those who earn $50K or more sing in the shower or bath, while only 20% of those who earn less than $20K do.

Fifty percent of the men and women who perceive themselves as overweight sing in the shower.

DO YOU APPLY SOAP DIRECTLY TO YOUR BODY OR LATHER UP YOUR HANDS FIRST?

AGE	LATHER		DIRECT	
	M	F	M	F
21-34	33	50	67	50
35-44	21	43	79	57
45-54	13	46	87	54
55 +	60	67	40	33
■ M □ F **M/F TOTALS**	20	47	80	53
GRAND TOTALS	31%		69%	

All numbers based on percentages.

Forty-three percent of the Southerners lather their hands first, while only 20% of the Northerners do.

Forty percent of those who earn $50K or more lather their hands first, while only 8% of those who earn less than $20K do.

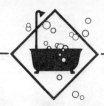

DO YOU POUR SHAMPOO DIRECTLY ONTO YOUR HEAD OR INTO YOUR HAND FIRST?

AGE	HEAD		HANDS	
	M	F	M	F
21-34	2	25	98	75
35-44	7	29	93	71
45-54	6	23	94	77
55 +	50	67	50	33
M/F TOTALS	9	26	91	74
GRAND TOTALS	16%		84%	

All numbers based on percentages.

Thirty-one percent of those earning $50K or more go right for the scalp with their shampoo, while only 8% of these earning $20K or less do.

DO YOU SQUEEZE THE TOOTHPASTE TUBE FROM THE TOP OR BOTTOM?

AGE	BOTTOM		TOP	
	M	F	M	F
21-34	37	33	63	67
35-44	33	43	67	57
45-54	10	30	90	70
55 +	10	45	90	55
M ■ F □	18	37	82	63
M/F TOTALS				
GRAND TOTALS	28%		72%	

All numbers based on percentages.

You can bet there are a lot of "his" and "her" toothpaste tubes around.

DO YOU OR YOUR MATE SPEND MORE TIME IN THE BATHROOM?

AGE	SELF		MATE	
	M	F	M	F
21-34	23	67	77	33
35-44	40	38	60	63
45-54	25	22	75	78
55+	50	25	50	75
■ M ☐ F M/F TOTALS			67	67
	33	33		
GRAND TOTALS	33%		67%	

All numbers based on percentages.

HOW MANY TIMES A WEEK DO YOU WEIGH YOURSELF?

AGE	NEVER		1X		2X		3X		4X +	
	M	F	M	F	M	F	M	F	M	F
21-34	22	62	46	30	25	2	4	4	3	2
35-44	50	45	32	41	4	2	11	1	3	11
45-54	28	38	22	36	1	7	26	11	23	8
55 +	26	34	23	6	2	30	13	1	36	29
■ M □ F **M/F TOTALS**	32	41	31	34	6	8	15	5	16	13
GRAND TOTALS	37%		33%		6%		10%		14%	

All numbers based on percentages.

AMERICANS AND
THEIR DECISIONS

DO YOU PREFER TO HEAR THE GOOD NEWS OR THE BAD NEWS FIRST?

AGE	GOOD		BAD	
	M	F	M	F
21-34	30	17	70	83
35-44	25	50	75	50
45-54	24	47	76	53
55 +	90	30	10	70
■ M □ F **M/F TOTALS**	32	40	68	60
GRAND TOTALS	**37%**		**63%**	

All numbers based on percentages.

Fifty-six percent of those who earn $50K or more like to hear the good news first.

Sixty-seven percent of those who earn less than $20K, Northerners (83%), Southerners (59%), college educated (76%) and non-college educated (53%) men and women want the bad news up front.

IF THERE IS A LARGE AND A SMALL PIECE OF PIE, WHICH ONE WOULD YOU KEEP?

AGE	BIGGER		SMALLER	
	M	F	M	F
21-34	98	33	2	67
35-44	44	23	56	77
45-54	45	34	55	66
55 +	98	17	2	83
■ M □ F **M/F TOTALS**	71	27	29	73
GRAND TOTALS	46%		54%	

All numbers based on percentages.

Sixty-three percent of the men who perceive themselves as overweight keep the bigger piece, while only 37% of the women who perceive themselves as overweight do.

Forty-five percent of the those earning less than $20K keep the bigger piece, while only 25% of those earning $50K or more do.

WHEN YOU GO OUT TO A THEATRE WITH ANOTHER COUPLE, IN WHAT ORDER DO YOU SIT?

AGE	M-F M-F		M-F F-M		F-M M-F		M-M F-F	
	M	F	M	F	M	F	M	F
21-34	44	31	2	66	50	2	4	1
35-44	19	23	78	70	2	6	1	1
45-54	24	33	47	56	12	3	18	8
55+	1	70	2	2	1	1	96	27
M/F TOTALS (■ M, □ F)	22	39	32	49	16	3	30	9
GRAND TOTALS	32%		43%		7%		18%	

All numbers based on percentages.

IF YOU SMOKE NOW OR EVER HAVE, HOW MANY TIMES HAVE YOU/DID YOU TRY TO QUIT?

AGE	NEVER		1X		2X		3X		4X +	
	M	F	M	F	M	F	M	F	M	F
21-34	2	1	1	30	1	16	2	15	94	38
35-44	1	5	16	15	13	29	23	20	47	31
45-54	1	4	18	38	19	27	16	14	46	17
55 +	1	2	6	11	8	14	4	29	81	44
M/F TOTALS	■ M □ F		1	2	12	23	10	22	11	20	66	33
GRAND TOTALS	2%		18%		17%		16%		47%	

All numbers based on percentages.

51

HAVE YOU EVER ENTERED A SWEEPSTAKES?

AGE	YES		NO	
	M	F	M	F
21-34	100	100	0	0
35-44	100	95	0	5
45-54	89	89	11	11
55 +	77	60	23	40
■ M □ F M/F TOTALS	89	88	11	12
GRAND TOTALS	88%		12%	

All numbers based on percentages.

Looks like Ed McMahon has more pull than most politicians.

HAVE YOU EVER BOUGHT A LOTTERY TICKET?

AGE	YES		NO	
	M	F	M	F
21-34	100	33	0	67
35-44	78	76	22	24
45-54	95	75	5	25
55 +	99	79	1	21
■ M □ F M/F TOTALS	92	71	8	29
GRAND TOTALS	79%		21%	

All numbers based on percentages.

HAVE YOU EVER PLACED A BET ON A SPORTING EVENT?

AGE	YES		NO	
	M	F	M	F
21-34	50	67	50	33
35-44	89	60	11	40
45-54	94	64	6	36
55 +	88	54	12	46
■ M ☐ F M/F TOTALS	87	61	13	39
GRAND TOTALS	70%		30%	

All numbers based on percentages.

DO YOU LICK THE FLAP
OF AN ENVELOPE FROM
LEFT TO RIGHT OR RIGHT TO LEFT?

AGE	L TO R		R TO L	
	M	F	M	F
21-34	76	67	24	33
35-44	73	75	27	25
45-54	65	60	35	40
55 +	75	73	25	27
■ M □ F M/F TOTALS	69	67	31	33
GRAND TOTALS	68%		32%	

All numbers based on percentages.

HOW OFTEN DO YOU BUCKLE YOUR SEAT BELT?

AGE	ALWAYS		SOME-TIMES		NEVER	
	M	F	M	F	M	F
21-34	62	90	33	8	5	2
35-44	62	71	31	22	7	7
45-54	55	57	29	33	15	10
55+	20	26	73	64	7	10
M/F TOTALS	57	66	34	26	9	8
GRAND TOTALS	61%		30%		9%	

■ M
□ F

All numbers based on percentages.

Compared to the total survey figure of 9%, more than twice as many Southerners (23%) never buckle up, with Northerners not much more responsible at 19%.

Seventy percent of the college educated respondents buckle up, while only 56% of the non-college respondents do.

White-collar workers exceed blue-collar workers in this safety precaution, 71% to 49%.

DO YOU GAS UP YOUR CAR WHEN IT IS 3/4 FULL, 1/2 EMPTY, 3/4 EMPTY OR ALMOST EMPTY?

AGE	¾ FULL		½ EMPTY		¾ EMPTY		ALMOST EMPTY	
	M	F	M	F	M	F	M	F
21-34	2	1	42	2	38	6	18	91
35-44	38	11	6	11	19	33	38	44
45-54	43	26	10	10	29	23	19	41
55 +	1	17	2	20	43	23	54	40
M/F TOTALS ■ M □ F	20	14	15	11	32	21	33	54
GRAND TOTALS	16%		12%		25%		47%	

All numbers based on percentages.

The college crowd (54%) and the Dixie drivers (47%) wait the longest to gas up.

Forty-four percent of those who earn $50K or more never let their tanks get below 3/4 full, while only 27% of those who earn less than $20K do.

WHICH SECTION OF THE NEWSPAPER DO YOU READ FIRST?

AGE	FRONT		BACK		FEATURE	
	M	F	M	F	M	F
21-34	60	46	7	9	33	45
35-44	66	40	7	18	27	42
45-54	58	53	6	14	36	33
55 +	40	60	7	8	53	32
M ■ / F □ M/F TOTALS	60	52	7	12	33	37
GRAND TOTALS	57%		9%		34%	

All numbers based on percentages.

Thirty-three percent of the Southerners and 69% of the Northerners read the front page of the newspaper first; 63% of the Southerners and 25% of the Northerners turn to a specific feature first.

Sixty-two percent of those who earn less than $20K begin with page one, while only 36% of those who earn $50K or more begin there; 23% of those who earn less than $20K turn directly to a specific article, while 62% of those who earn $50K or more do.

SINCE YOU HAVE BEEN ELIGIBLE, HAVE YOU VOTED IN AT LEAST ONE ELECTION A YEAR?

AGE	YES		NO	
	M	F	M	F
21-34	96	33	4	67
35-44	67	58	33	42
45-54	79	62	21	38
55 +	88	93	13	7
■ M □ F **M/F TOTALS**	77	62	23	38
GRAND TOTALS	**68%**		**32%**	

All numbers based on percentages.

More than half of the Southerners (53%) and half the college graduates (56%) did not bother to vote. Thirty-six percent of the Yanks stayed home, as did 28% of the non-college educated participants.

IF YOU FOUND A DIAMOND RING, WOULD YOU ATTEMPT TO LOCATE THE OWNER?

AGE	YES		NO	
	M	F	M	F
21-34	89	64	11	16
35-44	83	85	17	15
45-54	71	73	29	27
55 +	80	67	20	33
M/F TOTALS	79	79	21	21
GRAND TOTALS	79%		21%	

■ M □ F

All numbers based on percentages.

IF YOU FOUND A COIN ON THE PAVEMENT, WOULD YOU PICK IT UP?

AGE	YES		NO	
	M	F	M	F
21-34	93	93	7	7
35-44	75	94	25	6
45-54	98	90	2	10
55 +	98	73	2	27
M/F TOTALS	93	89	7	11
GRAND TOTALS	91%		9%	

All numbers based on percentages.

AMERICANS AND
THEIR CUISINE

WHEN PREPARING A PEANUT BUTTER AND JELLY SANDWICH, WHICH GOES ON TOP?

AGE	PB		JELLY	
	M	F	M	F
21-34	97	99	3	1
35-44	97	93	3	7
45-54	96	96	4	4
55 +	98	96	2	4
M F M/F TOTALS	98	94	2	6
GRAND TOTALS	96%		4%	

All numbers based on percentages.

DO YOU PUT PEANUT BUTTER ON THE SAME SLICE OF BREAD AS JELLY?

AGE	SAME		SEPARATE	
	M	F	M	F
21-34	93	25	7	75
35-44	60	86	40	14
45-54	46	72	54	28
55 +	92	90	8	10
■ M □ F M/F TOTALS	59	72	41	28
GRAND TOTALS	65%		35%	

All numbers based on percentages.

DO YOU EAT CORN ON THE COB SIDE-TO-SIDE OR IN CIRCLES?

AGE	SIDE		CIRCLES	
	M	F	M	F
21-34	33	10	67	90
35-44	18	21	82	79
45-54	17	27	83	73
55 +	10	33	90	67
■ M □ F M/F TOTALS	16	25	84	75
GRAND TOTALS	20%		80%	

All numbers based on percentages.

HOW MANY BOXES OF DIFFERENT CEREALS DO YOU HAVE?

AGE	NONE		1-2		3-4		5-6		7+	
	M	F	M	F	M	F	M	F	M	F
21-34	2	3	44	56	30	20	12	20	12	1
35-44	5	10	26	45	32	30	30	10	7	5
45-54	2	4	48	50	37	21	12	20	1	5
55 +	1	4	42	40	41	15	13	30	3	11
M/F TOTALS	3	5	40	48	35	21	17	20	5	6
GRAND TOTALS	4%		45%		26%		19%		6%	

M ■ F □

All numbers based on percentages.

DO YOU PUT KETCHUP DIRECTLY ON YOUR FRIES OR ALONGSIDE?

AGE	ON		SIDE	
	M	F	M	F
21-34	20	25	80	75
35-44	38	8	62	92
45-54	19	23	81	77
55 +	75	67	25	33
■ M □ F M/F TOTALS	26	22	74	78
GRAND TOTALS	24%		76%	

All numbers based on percentages.

Thirty-three percent of the white-collar workers splash the ketchup right on their fries, while only 12% of the blue-collar workers do.

DO YOU EAT THE DIFFERENT FOODS ON YOUR PLATE SEPARATELY OR MIXED TOGETHER?

AGE	SEPARATELY		TOGETHER	
	M	F	M	F
21-34	33	25	67	75
35-44	21	14	79	86
45-54	23	10	77	90
55+	30	17	70	83
■ M / □ F M/F TOTALS	20	11	80	89
GRAND TOTALS	16%		84%	

All numbers based on percentages.

Eighty-nine percent of the women and 16% of the men who consider themselves to be overweight graze on the entire plate at one time.

HOW DO YOU LIKE
YOUR STEAK COOKED?

AGE	RARE		MED		WELL	
	M	F	M	F	M	F
21-34	33	22	57	70	10	8
35-44	29	25	47	58	24	17
45-54	33	14	56	67	11	19
55 +	10	13	80	77	10	10
■ M □ F M/F TOTALS	32	18	53	67	15	15
GRAND TOTALS	26%		59%		15%	

All numbers based on percentages.

Thirteen percent of those who earn less than $20K like their meat rare, as opposed to 30% of those who earn $50K or more.

Forty-six percent of the Northerners like their meat bloody, as do 14% of the Southerners.

DO YOU EAT A SANDWICH COOKIE INTACT, OR DO YOU PULL IT APART AND EAT IT IN SEPARATE PIECES?

AGE	INTACT		PIECES	
	M	F	M	F
21-34	52	33	48	67
35-44	69	66	31	34
45-54	95	55	5	45
55+	99	65	1	35
■ M □ F M/F TOTALS	84	59	16	41
GRAND TOTALS	68%		32%	

All numbers based on percentages.

No matter how we pull apart the demographic stats, it seems most people eat their Oreos™ intact.

DO YOU APPLY EXTRA SALT TO YOUR FOOD?

AGE	YES		NO	
	M	F	M	F
21-34	10	50	90	50
35-44	62	50	38	50
45-54	52	40	48	60
55 +	40	67	60	33
■ M ☐ F M/F TOTALS	51	43	49	57
GRAND TOTALS	48%		52%	

All numbers based on percentages.

Sixty-three percent of the Southerners add salt to their food, while only 13% of the Northerners do.

IF YOU DO ADD SALT TO YOUR FOOD, DO YOU APPLY IT BEFORE YOU TASTE THE FOOD?

AGE	YES		NO	
	M	F	M	F
21-34	16	50	84	50
35-44	30	22	70	78
45-54	36	29	64	71
55 +	67	51	33	49
■ M ☐ F M/F TOTALS	35	33	65	67
GRAND TOTALS	34%		66%	

All numbers based on percentages.

Forty-eight percent of the Southerners and only 13% of the Northerners salt their food before tasting; Eastern residents rank the lowest at 13%.

Twenty-seven percent of the men and 28% of the women who perceive themselves as overweight salt indiscriminately.

WHEN MAKING HOT TEA, WHICH DO YOU PUT IN THE CUP FIRST, THE TEA BAG OR THE WATER?

AGE	TEA		WATER	
	M	F	M	F
21-34	52	98	48	2
35-44	47	67	53	33
45-54	48	68	52	32
55 +	48	99	52	1
■ M □ F M/F TOTALS	48	72	52	28
GRAND TOTALS	63%		38%	

All numbers based on percentages.

DO YOU EAT
YOUR FORTUNE COOKIE?

AGE	YES		NO	
	M	F	M	F
21-34	51	67	49	33
35-44	81	77	19	23
45-54	74	85	26	15
55 +	99	68	1	32
M / F TOTALS (■ M, □ F)	76	80	24	20
GRAND TOTALS	79%		21%	

All numbers based on percentages.

DO YOU EAT SPAGHETTI BY CUTTING IT OR BY WINDING IT AROUND YOUR FORK?

AGE	CUT		WIND	
	M	F	M	F
21-34	30	33	70	67
35-44	36	56	64	44
45-54	48	55	52	45
55 +	75	36	25	64
■ M ☐ F M/F TOTALS	46	48	54	52
GRAND TOTALS	47%		53%	

All numbers based on percentages.

Forty-four percent of the college educated and 53% of the non-college educated twirl their pasta.

Seventy-one percent of the men and 50% of the women who consider themselves to be overweight cut the stuff.

FOR REASONABLY GOOD SERVICE IN A RESTAURANT, WHAT KIND OF TIP WOULD YOU LEAVE?

AGE	5%		5-10%		11-15%		16-20%		20% +	
	M	F	M	F	M	F	M	F	M	F
21-34	3	1	52	1	30	96	14	1	1	1
35-44	1	5	37	32	39	40	12	14	11	9
45-54	5	5	43	13	50	60	1	19	1	3
55 +	4	3	49	56	4	28	42	10	1	3
M/F TOTALS (■ M / □ F)	3	4	45	26	31	55	17	11	4	4
GRAND TOTALS	4%		33%		47%		12%		4%	

All numbers based on percentages.

The biggest tippers live in the South (15.2% average), next are the Westerners (14% average), followed by the Easterners (13.6% average) and finally the Northerners (13.4% average).

Thirty-six percent of who earn less than $20K and 13% of those who earn $50K or more tip 10% or less.

Twice as many college graduates as non-graduates tip at 20%.

AMERICANS AND
THEIR MATES

DO YOU/DID YOU
LOVE YOUR MOTHER-IN-LAW?

AGE	YES		NO	
	M	F	M	F
21-34	99	99	1	1
35-44	99	61	1	39
45-54	86	78	14	22
55 +	71	75	29	25
■ M □ F M/F TOTALS	89 78		11 22	
GRAND TOTALS	84%		16%	

All numbers based on percentages.

It seems a lot of people were filling out the in-law questions under the scrutiny of their spouse.

DO YOU/DID YOU LOVE YOUR FATHER-IN-LAW?

AGE	YES		NO	
	M	F	M	F
21-34	99	67	1	33
35-44	89	72	11	28
45-54	88	75	12	25
55 +	76	50	24	50
■ M □ F M/F TOTALS	88	66	12	34
GRAND TOTALS	77%		23%	

All numbers based on percentages.

WOULD YOU MARRY YOUR SPOUSE AGAIN?

AGE	YES		NO	
	M	F	M	F
21-34	50	33	50	67
35-44	92	67	8	33
45-54	93	79	7	21
55 +	99	80	1	20
■ M / □ F / **M/F TOTALS**	90	72	10	28
GRAND TOTALS	**82%**		**18%**	

All numbers based on percentages.

Twenty-seven percent of the college educated and 14% of the non-college educated respondents would not repeat their vows.

While only 27% of those who earn less than $20K said they would not walk the aisle again, those earning $50K or more are split right down the middle.

HOW OFTEN DO YOU KISS YOUR SPOUSE GOOD NIGHT?

AGE	ALWAYS		USUALLY		RARELY		NEVER	
	M	F	M	F	M	F	M	F
21-34	50	36	43	10	2	52	5	2
35-44	74	29	12	36	10	29	3	7
45-54	44	48	25	38	29	10	2	5
55 +	74	41	23	43	2	10	1	6

M
F

M/F TOTALS	52	37	27	37	18	20	3	6
GRAND TOTALS	45%		32%		19%		4%	

All numbers based on percentages.

The cold weather must have gone to the Yank's hearts, only 25% usually kiss their spouse good night while 50% of the Southerners do.

HOW OFTEN DO YOU
KISS YOUR MATE WHEN LEAVING
THE HOUSE FOR THE DAY?

AGE	USUALLY		SOMETIMES		NEVER	
	M	F	M	F	M	F
21-34	67	75	3	5	30	20
35-44	69	60	24	30	7	10
45-54	62	65	36	22	2	13
55 +	60	58	39	36	1	6
■ M □ F M/F TOTALS	66	63	30	20	4	17
GRAND TOTALS	65%		26%		9%	

All numbers based on percentages.

Notice the difference between the male total and the female total in the "NEVER" column. Talk about perception versus reality!

HOW MANY TIMES A DAY DO YOU HAVE LOVING THOUGHTS ABOUT YOUR MATE?

AGE	NEVER		1-2		3-5		6-10		11 +	
	M	F	M	F	M	F	M	F	M	F
21-34	16	8	18	29	50	33	10	20	6	10
35-44	8	4	24	21	32	34	8	16	28	25
45-54	5	3	21	17	27	22	5	10	42	48
55 +	4	1	7	4	32	25	11	17	46	53
■ M □ F M/F TOTALS	2	3	13	13	39	29	10	13	36	42
GRAND TOTALS	2%		13%		35%		12%		38%	

All numbers based on percentages.

Twenty-one- to thirty-four-year-olds aren't too romantic. It's obvious they come from the "Me" generation.

DO YOU AND YOUR MATE TEND TO AGREE ON POLITICAL ISSUES?

AGE	YES		NO	
	M	F	M	F
21-34	11	43	89	57
35-44	28	27	72	73
45-54	35	25	65	75
55 +	60	11	40	89
■ M □ F M/F TOTALS	32	26	68	74
GRAND TOTALS	29%		71%	

All numbers based on percentages.

Looks like a lot of couples can't even agree to disagree. However, 81% of the Southern couples and 57% of the Northern couples would vote with their mate.

DO YOU HAVE MORE FRIENDS THAN YOUR MATE?

AGE	YES		NO	
	M	F	M	F
21-34	50	34	50	66
35-44	67	17	33	83
45-54	27	50	73	50
55 +	50	25	50	75
■ M □ F **M/F TOTALS**	41	35	59	65
GRAND TOTALS	37%		63%	

All numbers based on percentages.

Ninety-two percent of the Southern women have more friends than their mates. It's a much closer tie in the North, with men having more friends, 55%-45%.

Whether the couple is rich or poor, they're split 50%-50% on who has more friends.

WHEN YOU AND YOUR MATE SEND A GREETING CARD, WHOSE NAME IS SIGNED FIRST?

AGE	HIS		HERS	
	M	F	M	F
21-34	67	80	33	20
35-44	64	64	36	36
45-54	75	78	25	22
55 +	33	67	67	33
■ M □ F **M/F TOTALS**	69	72	31	28
GRAND TOTALS	**69%**		**31%**	

All numbers based on percentages.

The East is the most traditional segment of the country in this regard with 80% of the men signing a card first; the South proved to be the least traditional with only 58% opting for his name first on dual greetings.

WHO TAKES OUT THE GARBAGE IN YOUR HOUSEHOLD?

AGE	HE		SHE	
	M	F	M	F
21-34	67	90	33	10
35-44	92	63	8	38
45-54	90	63	10	38
55 +	80	63	20	37
■ M □ F M/F TOTALS	89	67	11	33
GRAND TOTALS	80%		20%	

All numbers based on percentages.

Seems roles haven't changed much in the sanitation department.

DO YOU SHOP ALONE OR WITH YOUR MATE?

AGE	ALONE		MATE	
	M	F	M	F
21-34	67	25	33	75
35-44	31	46	69	54
45-54	42	63	58	37
55 +	60	94	40	6
■ M □ F M/F TOTALS	48	57	52	43
GRAND TOTALS	53%		47%	

All numbers based on percentages.

Only the 21- to 34-year-old men prefer to shop without their mates. This allows them, no doubt, to buy all the Twinkies™ they want.

WHOSE MESSAGE IS ON
YOUR ANSWERING MACHINE?

AGE	HIS		HERS	
	M	F	M	F
21-34	97	80	3	20
35-44	78	58	22	42
45-54	73	53	27	47
55 +	60	71	40	29
■ M □ F **M/F TOTALS**	78	60	22	40
GRAND TOTALS	64%		36%	

All numbers based on percentages.

There's some kind of power struggle going on with the 21-34 age group. Both males and females take credit for having their greeting on the family answering machine.

WHO IS USUALLY LATE IN YOUR HOUSEHOLD?

AGE	HE		SHE		BOTH	
	M	F	M	F	M	F
21-34	57	20	29	60	14	20
35-44	40	27	40	64	20	9
45-54	61	34	33	37	6	29
55 +	33	56	65	33	2	11
M/F TOTALS	53	35	38	45	9	20
GRAND TOTALS	41%		41%		18%	

■ M

□ F

All numbers based on percentages.

According to this survey, the more educated a man is, the more prompt he is. Only 25% of the college educated men, as opposed to 45% of the non-college educated men, were named as the culprits.

WHO GENERALLY APOLOGIZES FIRST IN YOUR HOUSEHOLD?

AGE	HE		SHE	
	M	F	M	F
21-34	69	33	31	67
35-44	64	47	36	53
45-54	57	70	43	30
55+	50	80	50	20
M ■ F □ M/F TOTALS	59	62	41	38
GRAND TOTALS	60%		40%	

All numbers based on percentages.

America has its humblest generation yet; both men and women in the 21-34 age group claim to be the first to apologize.

According to the women, the older men get, the more time they spend on their knees.

DO YOU WEAR A WEDDING RING?

AGE	YES		NO	
	M	F	M	F
21-34	68	60	32	40
35-44	82	54	18	46
45-54	78	61	22	39
55 +	50	56	50	44
■ M □ F M/F TOTALS	76	58	24	42
GRAND TOTALS	67%		33%	

All numbers based on percentages.

DOES YOUR SPOUSE WEAR A WEDDING RING?

AGE	YES		NO	
	M	F	M	F
21-34	40	80	60	20
35-44	55	80	45	20
45-54	37	70	63	30
55+	50	73	50	27
■ M □ F M/F TOTALS	46	75	54	25
GRAND TOTALS	63%		37%	

All numbers based on percentages.

AMERICANS AND THEIR BODIES

DO YOU LIKE THE WAY YOU LOOK IN THE NUDE?

AGE	YES		NO	
	M	F	M	F
21-34	90	33	10	67
35-44	67	30	33	70
45-54	56	14	44	86
55 +	88	40	13	60
■ M □ F M/F TOTALS	68	22	32	78
GRAND TOTALS	41%		59%	

All numbers based on percentages.

Fifty-five percent of the men and 59% of the women who perceive themselves as overweight say they like the way they look in the buff.

ARE YOU PLEASED WITH YOUR APPEARANCE IN CLOTHES?

AGE	YES		NO	
	M	F	M	F
21-34	94	67	6	33
35-44	89	74	11	26
45-54	89	64	11	36
55 +	91	60	9	40
■ M □ F M/F TOTALS	92	65	8	35
GRAND TOTALS	72%		24%	

All numbers based on percentages.

HOW OFTEN DO YOU CLEAN YOUR BELLYBUTTON?

AGE	DAILY		WEEKLY		MONTHLY		FEW Xs A YEAR		NEVER	
	M	F	M	F	M	F	M	F	M	F
21-34	40	23	3	47	3	4	4	20	50	6
35-44	53	40	13	15	3	10	6	20	25	15
45-54	26	39	37	25	11	8	5	8	21	20
55 +	48	20	3	40	31	5	2	16	16	19
M/F TOTALS (■ M □ F)	42	31	14	31	12	7	4	16	28	15
GRAND TOTALS	38%		26%		7%		10%		20%	

All numbers based on percentages.

DO YOU KNOW
YOUR CHOLESTEROL COUNT?

AGE	YES		NO	
	M	F	M	F
21-34	2	2	98	98
35-44	25	18	75	82
45-54	52	39	48	61
55 +	2	64	98	36
■ M ☐ F **M/F TOTALS**	36	34	64	66
GRAND TOTALS	**36%**		**64%**	

All numbers based on percentages.

DID YOU EVER BITE YOUR FINGERNAILS?

AGE	YES		NO	
	M	F	M	F
21-34	98	98	2	2
35-44	82	98	18	2
45-54	97	92	3	8
55 +	96	60	4	40
M/F TOTALS	91	92	9	8
GRAND TOTALS	92%		8%	

M
F

All numbers based on percentages.

It's surprising there is a nail manicurist with a client under 55.

DID YOU EVER BITE YOUR TOENAILS?

AGE	YES		NO	
	M	F	M	F
21-34	4	33	96	67
35-44	25	43	75	57
45-54	25	21	75	79
55 +	3	17	97	83
■ M □ F M/F TOTALS	21	28	79	72
GRAND TOTALS	25%		75%	

All numbers based on percentages.

Wouldn't you love to have a photo of those toenail biters in action?

DO YOU CRACK YOUR KNUCKLES?

AGE	YES		NO	
	M	**F**	**M**	**F**
21-34	10	50	90	50
35-44	17	25	83	75
45-54	14	10	86	90
55 +	75	10	25	90
■ M □ F **M/F TOTALS**	21	19	79	81
GRAND TOTALS	**20%**		**80%**	

All numbers based on percentages.

DO YOU TWIDDLE YOUR THUMBS?

AGE	YES		NO	
	M	F	M	F
21-34	1	1	99	99
35-44	11	1	89	99
45-54	24	4	76	96
55+	1	19	99	81
■ M ☐ F **M/F TOTALS**			86	95
	14	5		
GRAND TOTALS	**8%**		**92%**	

All numbers based on percentages.

DO YOU HAVE A REGIONAL ACCENT?

AGE	YES		NO	
	M	F	M	F
21-34	52	67	48	33
35-44	25	38	75	62
45-54	48	35	52	65
55 +	2	17	98	83
M/F TOTALS	38	35	62	65
GRAND TOTALS	37%		63%	

All numbers based on percentages.

Seventy-five percent of those who earn $50K or more deny having any special speech pattern; 50% of those who earn less than $20K profess to speak with a distinct regional accent.

DO YOU SPEAK ANY OTHER LANGUAGE(S) BESIDES ENGLISH?

AGE	NONE		1		2 +	
	M	F	M	F	M	F
21-34	67	67	33	33	0	0
35-44	70	50	30	33	0	17
45-54	64	83	36	13	0	4
55 +	88	84	11	15	1	1
M ■ / F □ / M/F TOTALS	69	71	26	19	5	9
GRAND TOTALS	70%		23%		7%	

All numbers based on percentages.

The North and South are tied at 84% of each population not speaking any other language than English. Twelve percent of the Southerners speak more than one language and 9% of the Northerners do. Seven percent of the Northerners speak more than two languages, while 4% of the Southerners do.

CAN YOU WHISTLE BY INSERTING YOUR FINGERS IN YOUR MOUTH?

AGE	YES		NO	
	M	F	M	F
21-34	4	50	96	50
35-44	33	15	67	85
45-54	21	18	79	82
55+	13	2	88	98
■ M ☐ F **M/F TOTALS**	21	16	79	84
GRAND TOTALS	17%		83%	

All numbers based on percentages.

It seems 21- to 34-year-old females can wolf-whistle better than their male counterparts.

HAVE YOU EVER BEEN OUTSIDE THE CONTINENTAL UNITED STATES?

AGE	YES		NO	
	M	F	M	F
21-34	99	66	1	34
35-44	93	59	7	41
45-54	91	75	9	25
55 +	99	83	1	17
■ M ☐ F M/F TOTALS	93	71	7	29
GRAND TOTALS	79%		21%	

All numbers based on percentages.

As might be expected, those who earn less than $20K are more U.S. bound than any other group.

Sixty-nine percent of the total of 21% stay-at-homes are from below the Mason-Dixon line. Perhaps Southern comfort can't be beat.

HAVE YOU EVER VISITED WASHINGTON, D.C.?

AGE	YES		NO	
	M	F	M	F
21-34	86	75	14	25
35-44	66	71	34	29
45-54	58	43	42	57
55 +	40	67	60	33
M ■ / F □ M/F TOTALS	63	57	37	43
GRAND TOTALS	60%		40%	

All numbers based on percentages.

Southerners (77%) and Northerners (75%) seem to be more interested in the White House than Westerners (53%) and Easterners (49%).

HAVE YOU EVER BEEN TO DISNEYLAND OR DISNEY WORLD?

AGE	YES		NO	
	M	F	M	F
21-34	90	53	10	47
35-44	79	71	21	29
45-54	68	60	32	40
55+	80	33	20	67
■ M □ F M/F TOTALS	76	62	24	38
GRAND TOTALS	70%		30%	

All numbers based on percentages.

More people go see Mickey Mouse than the nation's capitol. If they only knew how much Mickey Mouse is there, too.

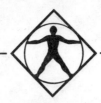

DO YOU CONSIDER YOURSELF
TO BE A SUPERSTITIOUS PERSON?

AGE	YES		NO	
	M	F	M	F
21-34	50	25	50	75
35-44	21	31	79	69
45-54	29	47	71	53
55+	10	12	90	88
M/F TOTALS	25	37	75	63
GRAND TOTALS	30%		70%	

■ M
□ F

All numbers based on percentages.

It seems the older we get, the less superstitious we are. (Knock on wood!)

DO YOU BELIEVE IN REINCARNATION?

AGE	YES		NO	
	M	F	M	F
21-34	96	70	4	30
35-44	34	38	64	62
45-54	13	48	87	52
55 +	46	33	54	57
M/F TOTALS	28	44	72	56
GRAND TOTALS	35%		65%	

All numbers based on percentages.

Forty-two percent of college educated people believe in reincarnation; only 30% of the non-college educated believe.

Forty-six percent of those earning $50K or more believe in a comeback, while only 33% percent of those who earn less than $20K do.

WERE YOU AFRAID OF THE DARK AS A CHILD?

AGE	YES		NO	
	M	**F**	**M**	**F**
21-34	52	99	48	1
35-44	48	68	52	32
45-54	29	45	71	55
55 +	51	54	49	46
■ M □ F **M/F TOTALS**	45	67	55	33
GRAND TOTALS	**60%**		**40%**	

All numbers based on percentages.

ARE YOU AFRAID OF THE DARK NOW?

AGE	YES		NO	
	M	F	M	F
21-34	1	2	99	98
35-44	20	22	80	78
45-54	1	24	99	76
55 +	48	1	52	99
■ M □ F M/F TOTALS	12	19	88	81
GRAND TOTALS	17%		83%	

All numbers based on percentages.

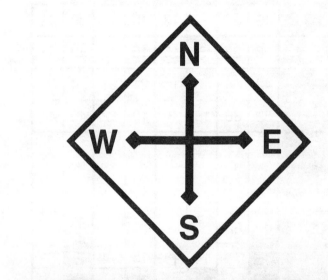

AMERICAN SURVEY
DEMOGRAPHICS

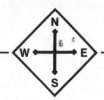

AGE & SEX

AGE	NORTH		SOUTH		EAST		WEST	
	M	F	M	F	M	F	M	F
21-34	19	32	29	13	13	13	39	42
35-44	28	22	8	15	15	10	49	53
45-54	42	34	13	10	21	21	24	35
55+	32	36	18	8	10	12	40	44
M/F TOTALS (■ M, □ F)	35	30	14	12	15	14	36	44
GRAND TOTALS	32%		13%		14%		41%	

All numbers based on percentages.

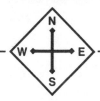

INCOME

HOUSEHOLD INCOME	NORTH	SOUTH	EAST	WEST	TOTAL
LESS THAN 20K	7	6	9	17	**11%**
20-29K	34	30	33	39	**34%**
30-49K	47	47	52	33	**44%**
50K +	12	17	6	11	**11%**

All numbers based on percentages.

OCCUPATION

OCCUPATION	NORTH	SOUTH	EAST	WEST	TOTAL
WHITE-COLLAR	53	61	45	46	**50%**
BLUE-COLLAR	47	39	55	54	**50%**

All numbers based on percentages.

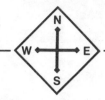

EDUCATION

EDUCATION	NORTH	SOUTH	EAST	WEST	TOTAL
H. S. OR LESS	7	23	2	2	**8%**
H. S. GRADUATE	71	35	80	71	**65%**
SOME COLLEGE	20	40	12	17	**22%**
COLLEGE GRADUATE	2	3	6	10	**6%**

All numbers based on percentages.

AGE OF MATE

AGE	NORTH		SOUTH		EAST		WEST	
	M	F	M	F	M	F	M	F
OLDER	96	31	81	45	80	46	94	28
YOUNGER	4	69	19	55	20	54	6	72

All numbers based on percentages.

NUMBER OF TIMES MARRIED

# TIMES MARRIED	NORTH	SOUTH	EAST	WEST
0	7	7	9	7
1X	79	80	62	72
2X	14	13	26	17
3X+	0	0	3	4

All numbers based on percentages.

NUMBER OF CHILDREN

# OF CHILDREN	NORTH	SOUTH	EAST	WEST
0	17	6	14	11
1	9	20	13	17
2	37	42	48	23
3	18	14	9	13
4	11	11	9	31
5+	8	7	7	5

All numbers based on percentages.

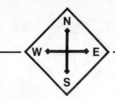

PERCEIVED WEIGHT

WEIGHT	NORTH		SOUTH		EAST		WEST		TOTAL
	M	F	M	F	M	F	M	F	
OVER	54	74	60	63	57	59	52	64	**60%**
AVERAGE	36	18	29	34	28	32	38	30	**31%**
UNDER	10	8	11	3	15	9	10	6	**9%**

All numbers based on percentages.

PERCEIVED HEIGHT

PERCEIVED HEIGHT	NORTH		SOUTH		EAST		WEST		TOTAL
	M	F	M	F	M	F	M	F	
ABOVE AVERAGE	24	13	16	10	22	10	14	14	**16%**
AVERAGE	67	68	78	77	67	71	71	66	**68%**
BELOW AVERAGE	9	19	6	13	11	19	15	20	**16%**

All numbers based on percentages.